Stephen —
best of friends

BRAVEST AT MIDNIGHT

David

a collection of poems

"These were not tepid stars of torpid places
But bravest at midnight and in lonely spaces..."
~Wallace Stevens, "Page from a Tale," from *The Auroras of Autumn*

DAVID ZUCKER

* * * * *

Disclaimer
This is a work of fiction, a product of the author's imagination. Any resemblance or similarity to any actual events or persons, living or dead, is purely coincidental.

* * * * *

Cover Photo Courtesy of Shutterstock.com
Formatting and cover design by Debora Lewis arenapublishing.org

ISBN-13: 978-1530232192
ISBN-10: 1530232198

For Betsey Parlato

Thanks go to these magazines and collections for publishing some of these poems, some in different form.

Chattahoochee Review: "Housebound"

Chelsea: "An Album"

Connecticut River Review: "The Door"

Embers: "Mad in Italy," "Sands of Iwo Jima"

Free Inquiry: "The Shape of Desiring"

Graham House Review: "Encountering Henry *Moore's* Nudes in Public Places"

Greenfield Review: "In Memory of Antoine de St. Exupéry," "Late November," "Lines While Drunk," "Ohio Towns"

Portals: A College Reader, ed. William Brown and Mary Segall (Harcourt Brace, 1998):"My Father"

Limestone: "At the Desk"

Midwest Poetry Review: "A Name"

Occident: "The Ivory Gate"

Panache: "Reading the Talmud at 3 A.M," "Origin Obscure"

Present Tense: "Bible Story"

Quinnipiac/Schweitzer Journal: "A Hillside Saunter"

Shenandoah: "Thunderbolt"

Shirim: "Entrance to the Old Cracow Ghetto"; Reprinted in *Blood to Remember: American Poets on the Holocaust,* ed. Charles Fishman (Texas Tech University Press,1991)

The Threepenny Review: "Moriah"

Webster Review: "New Faces"

CONTENTS

I

THE ART OF OUR NECESSITIES

"The art of our necessities is strange,
That can make vile things precious."

~*King Lear*, Act 3, scene 2

1

I always, or sometimes,
appear to collapse
into some spinning
center of chaos.

That may be where
my stripped nature
began, and must rest.
The near-blind search,
ordering of words

by poets with the blunt
tooth of hungry feeling,
can't be all that goads
our wanting, though
we do long for black

strong straight lines.
This longing must find
our being in a far-from-us,
in an alien run-of-the-mill,
unsuspected by thinking, saying.

2

I saw a shrunk bent man
riffling through the food bins—
his body so broken, birth
botched, his tiny face all fiery
bumps. I could not tell

how he could avoid
even polite humiliations
in his day's dragging time.
My sickened furtive stare
turned me in fear for myself,

for pity was locked,
buried within me,
flooded with terror
at the broken in their multitudes
and my mysterious flushed health.

3

The long yacht in bright sheen
slipped past the huddled
homeless on the wide
river on a clear night
as a glistening woman

at the railing wept for them,
for herself, for her carefree
companions, as a blank bright
harvest moon kept watch.

AT A POETRY READING

Prison house shadows linger
in florescent glow and hum.
We are here to see, be seen, be known,
to hope this voice could be echoing
our own, could lend us voice,
polish our rasping every day.

All a mistake. He follows
A plan in how to say and sound,
as if language itself kept school.
We are filed, swept into corners,
we, a mystery, yet so clear,
bread and honey on a white cloth.

His voice drifts over us, a wash
of newness in floods of change,
our hearts hooded by masks of false feeling.
True poets don't give answers
for our pain together, or pain alone.

Their voices enter us by streams
running too swift to drink,
yet enter to warm our chill.
They come from a journey as guests,
familiars for a night, but not ours.
We know them as we hear them,

as we hear a distant sea rush,
as Ariel was heard by the well-bred son
who wandered into the island's dreaming.

Unilingual

Of all the prisons
enclosing me
this one holds me
tightest.

I know no words
that can tell me–
except smatterings
of others–

what it is I see
and hear and taste,
my one conduit
a koan giving

another mystery,
another clarity.
I cannot help

but be caressed by it–
like a soft embrace
of your smooth arms.
This prison makes hard

demands, holds me
accountable, gives
hints and flashes for what
I dimly know

yet lavishes on me
over and over.

DOUBLE EXPOSURE: INSTRUCTIONS FOR A POEM
(From Diane Arbus)

She is trying to tell me something,
not mystical... aesthetic, practical.
She stretches her thin hands upward,
stares with her wide dreaming-keen eyes,
the apertures readjusting to the thriving,
inward-looking, companionable oddities,
unfit perhaps but fit to her own scheme of things.

In the Middle Ages she and her poet brother
would be mystics in Jewish Russia.
Her glamorous yet still and simple presence
(in the dozen or so photos of her), connecting her
to her chosen corners of the city's waste places,
strangely distant outside the frame, not wanting
to join her subjects, almost all she "liked."

She had hopes their mysteries could be hers
if she looked and took their pictures then choosing
the right ones from contact sheets, watching
the ghosts rise from her darkroom
(dark, in at least a double sense).
I imagine her talking to me as
she might have talked to her brother:

"Learn first to see, as I got the strange hang of it.
Approach them in non-condescending fashion,
allow them to want you to observe them,
accept your camera as part of you,
part of your friendly curiosity, even let them
take your picture. Let them like your observing them,
move just far enough away to go inside their muted
off-center lives–no weirder, better or worse than yours–
to have them trust you, then push the shutter.
Make them an extension of your hand,
your eye, never sentimental or indulgent . . .
let their curiosity for you become yours of them.
Such interchange will show in your poem as at best
it shows in my photos. Put all anxiousness for meanings

out of mind. Don't grasp for soul, not even mine,
and let the world's body be your companion, yes, let it be
your body, and gently touch yourself to confirm the connection–
like bumping into a wall, so your problem is solved!
Check in to make sure it is there for you, your presence
and theirs together in your short or long lives.
Let it be with you the thing itself.

Please don't reach to explain my suicide.
I was very depressed (my burden, my chemistry).
You could say I suddenly . . .
Well, it was like fondling a new camera.
I wanted to abandon the daily round.
I think those I knew well understood.

Look at the last photos of me, how good
I looked (or from fashion-shoot days' lingo,
"beautiful," "stunning"), my thin angles
a bit like my subjects, more worn... more
remote but alert, I was always alert.

Know how I loved my life, the city, the wasted
interiors (only apparently), the streets, my cameras,
the Jewish giant and his parents (not sad, attentive),
the home for the retarded (not sad, playful)...
most of all my darkroom, a refuge where
surprised like a child as the ghostly images
rose before me—startling, fresh, new!—
from the bath of life-releasing chemicals.
All the solid and odd bodies, desires
because I waited for them...

You have to know I wasn't that important.
I was the medium at a séance. Now as bodies
they're gone, even their shadows have shadows.
They rise as I caress them in their bath water
as I would babies... my rubber gloves, my tongs,
hunting for the right soft paper for them.

How nourishing the darkness could be.
I never loved anything so much
since I learned how to mix the chemicals,
use the old enlarger. I sealed off the streets
(I loved sounds as well as images)...
The red light around my long model's fingers,
turning the printer knobs like a bombardier adjusting his sights,
like a mother pinning diapers on the clothesline,
spacing my prints to air dry. The cloud-gradations
of white and black, why I never used color...
I loved light before it broke up into the spectrum.
How I came to look and remember.

Go then, feel the full surfaces these things
and people in your own quiet my photos gave,
sufficient unto themselves... Maybe you can
grasp my wispiness if you look at the world as it is.
Be ready to readjust so very slightly
your own camera, your darkroom.
Be ever so attentive, as in the light when
the images glow in my darkened room

with the ripple in the trays, the prints drying
with the smallest flutter. Look at them,
stroke them with your eyes,
let your words take on my eyes.
Don't search for word-shapes, sounds.
They will arrive in silence behind your eyes...

Oh, best to leave the exhibit book behind."

A NAME

I thought I knew her name
from a party list or a driver
license dropped on the road.
Ten years later I saw her name

spilled out for officials
in a document fingered,
stained, filed, not blessed by
her corrections,

seeping from the accidents
of looking then losing.

My loss turned rust under
the gloss of the newly painted,
whatever I want to lend luster.

The Name and the Rose

How we have pruned excess
from each other,
like children trimming names
to rhyming chants and scales.

We have bared ourselves
to flecked and quivering skin,
as tumbling with our wanting.

We try to yank our flesh away
from chattering emulations,
until the rose's hidden center
opens to a poised mocking.

Sometimes I only hear my rant.
Sometimes we sleepwalk, leaving
the firelit room to climb in silence
to the attic's secrets. Then we go down

to breathe each other's skin,
hear our sleeping breath,
know more than we can hope
of the night-gathered silent rose.

SIX SMALL ROSES

One whimpered, petiteness her shrill theme,
"I am so... incomplete, so very small."

A second, blazing in self-pride, babbled
on her branching form and grace.

A third, enfolded from the others,
hardly spoke, fixed on an empty center.

The fourth, new puffed with certainty,
flushed pink, violet, damask flourishes.

A budded fifth, burrowed within
herself, stoked aglow her brief youth.

The sixth and dearest, often dark
in doubt, gained fresh hope
in stretching toward her

non-rose other while he wondered
daily at her beauty, ardor, merit.

TWO ROSES

Rummaging for metaphors
the poet bends to his pen.
The roses know nothing of
The word-ways he strains for.
The roses perhaps know
the other loves her

for her color, her way of
opening with or without
the sun–a harkening, a habit,
trusting the sun will be there.
She opens with a small blush
to the warmth. So the poet imagines
each bends toward the other.

By such gradual motions,
they keep to their purposes,
willing to stand in water,
to follow after light.

II

A HILLSIDE SAUNTER

"...sauntering: which word is beautifully derived "from idle people who roved about the country, in the Middle Ages, and asked charity, under pretence of going à la Sainte Terre, *to the Holy Land..."*

Henry David Thoreau, Walking

(In memory of Chris Becker, who died by fire)

A hillside walk cools and tires
a motley of friends and family of one
dead from fire, scholar to this mountain,
to wildflowers, streams, peoples, tongues.
As the sun climbs obliquely
we find a laureled, scrub pined path,
through basalt refined in primordial fire,
our burden a can of ashes.

The forced gaiety of graveyard chatter,
the brightening March afternoon,
grow lighter. A sunbathed hillside greets us,
a valley stretches beneath.
We stagger our saying like Quakers.
Hikers pass politely, their shoes
against stone a blunted music.

Many kinds of love pass through spring air:
seasoned, new blazes, old embers,
all refining the man's bright coin.
The mountain gives solace after a bitter winter.

We throw the ashes into a sudden gust
Whitening us in blowback.

17

My Father
(Died February 6, 1969)

After so long
no clear remembrance
no reconciliation
no clarified friendship

Also no rancor
no gasp for the last words
no anger with desperate aim
no stumbling reunion

Instead–refreshment
in others he never saw
longing for some he spoke of
all those by his presence

larger than behind
his armchair
where on tiptoe
I combed his thick dark hair

THE BICYCLE

I got it through my father's efforts. During the war bicycles were impossible to buy new, almost as hard to get used. One day he had a tip on a rebuilt bike so we drove to a cluttered shop on Carnegie Avenue. Before the car was parked, a squat red bike glowed in the window. I could see rust. But the silver fenders and the sweep of the handlebars, with leather tassels sprouting from the rubber handle bar grips! The man who sold it was swarthy and hairy, wearing a clean undershirt. I told my father how much I liked the bike. He paid the man, who made a few adjustments with his pocketful of wrenches. We drove away with the prize, front wheel protruding from the trunk. I rode the bike self-consciously the block while kids my age stared enviously. My father glowed with the triumph of difficult acquisition.

The above is a sentimentalized version of a harsher fact in the life of a boy and his father. The photo which the paragraph elaborates suggests nothing, of course, of narrative, certainly not the suburban heart-warmer. The photo shows, in crinkled black and white, a dull little bike, a boy of seven holding the handlebars while standing at an angle midway between bars and seat, and in the background a glum thirty-five year old man, with no discernible emotion or thought; he does exude a brooding authoritative presence. The man is bored, perhaps distracted, overworked, anxious about the draft, although it is unlikely that he'll be called up. The photo is dated 1944, the same year some remote cousins of the father's, whom no one in the family had heard from or about for decades, may have been converted to greasy smoke in some death factory in Poland. I suppose anyone can see the similarities in the features and assume they are father and son. A few more essential details. The garage is open, showing

19

the family car with sullen-faced grill, some gardening tools. The yard shows vaguely a line of shrubs, a large elm tree hovering near the father. The boy seems to be looking directly into the camera; the father's gaze is angled more toward the house, whose side door is just visible in the left corner of the frame.

~~~

The energy pulsates beyond the street into the city roasting in summer. The heat crushes everyone but the boy and his father who have escaped through the photo into the release of forty years. They are gazers in forgetfulness too, in their surrender to the moment. The grayish paint of the garage is probably red or green. The boy's shirt is probably blue, the father's high, loose trousers brown. The mother must looks with pride and concern, knowing that the memories are waiting when her husband is gone from her, when the son is older than his father is now and time has burned all away but the light and the shadow the man and the boy and the bicycle have cast. The mother and father, both dead now, seem impossibly alive. Even more, American, despite the horror that is unfolding across the ocean. A nephew has just taken off from a Yorkshire base to bomb German supply lines in Czechoslovakia. Forty years later he realizes his squadron could have easily dropped its bombs on the I.G. Farben factories 100 miles away at Auschwitz.

~~~

Haven't you sat hushed before your own albums–speculating, imagining? Haven't the secret codes made their way into your consciousness? Nothing so rebukes the materiality of our lives than the ghostliness of the box of photos. They glow like steel vaults of our casual investment in a consumable immortality.

~~~

The American family shows its self-consciousness easily. Every member of the boy's family has "felt" ~~completes~~ those years when looking at this snapshot from my father's old bellows Kodak. I was four and do not remember the occasion, except a hazy sense of being hovered over. The odor of the food lingers to this day. The wooden table centers the picture. A small garage on the right casts a shadow. It looks like a house: side window, hinged front doors (before the era of the overhead). More like a barn than a garage, it reflects the small town origins of half this family... One almost expects horses to stamp and steam. The table is still loaded with food, no paper plates but china, and a pot of beans and franks, sauerkraut, potato salad. I am in front. My mother's hand rests on my shoulder. My father is behind us, his arm around my sister, comforting her after she seems to have just had a cry.

~~~

This reading of the photo is right on an emotional target. It leaves out one crucial matter. In the upper right of the photo is a young man, a cousin, who pouts and is clearly outside the family circle. He and a slim young woman on the front bench may have quarreled. Her face is turned towards him, looking at him with either rage or lust. Her glance has haunted me ever since. ~~The~~ *She* almost seems to be an unidentified saint in a corner of a triptych.

~~~

The Softball Game

The softball game mingles with the wood of the picnic table. The game itself is recorded in four photos. I suspect there were more but assembled they have vanished. One photo shows the family at the picnic. My father is on the mound in the small diamond in the schoolyard across the street. He looks at the batter, another cousin, a large man, an ex-Seebee beginning to show the fat that in later years engulfed him. My sister is the catcher and is obviously afraid of the bat and fouled balls. My father stares implacably as she turns to retrieve the ball. The other three photos record a few other changes in the unknown and of course inconsequential course of the game: someone running to third, my father staring into center field, probably after a ball. What is remarkable is the background. No one else is present, only this family at its game. In the third photo one can see another game in the background. You can detect a surrender the symmetry of their game. They concentrate. They are out of themselves almost as if they are seeing into the permanence of the album.

~~~

The comments above have their charm but become excessively mystical and, finally, sentimental. The truth is... well, my interpretation is quite different. Of course, most will say any "interpretation" at all is irrelevant. The snapshot records, quite vaguely, a purely personal family gathering which has no meaning to anyone outside the family. The softball game can be noted as a Type like a million others of its kind. A post-modernist critic might comment on a mythicizing of American common life. These comments move slightly in that direction. I like the configuration of the players, their shadows cast toward dark masses of trees on the right side. The photos have some interesting "accidents of form." It is unnecessary to speculate more.

~~~

The snapshots shine with simple memory. The light spills, shadows drift.

~(Frank O'Hara, "Sleeping on the Wing")

It's breaking-out time too long delayed.
Lives at work and play are dead or dying.
A lost language out of new-polished tombstones
near the Hamden dump across the street,
the Puritan past's stones down the block.

The lives all around look sick-sleepy
and my own isn't as pert as it was wont to be
long hours of the day which grow blank and calm
not as can be expected in a head so keyed to sparkling
surface signals from fine green eyes at the grocer's

Out looking to bring up the spirits from the deep
all ghosts are good enough just keep them rising
like termites on the wing fluttering and spooking
breaking into their supermarket shuffle and gaze
where the bright colored soaps and imported goods keep watch

Out reaching Hondas streaming everywhere wondering
where they're all going with so many not working
four new pasta salad shops on the avenues in six months
so many are eating well the wide world's offerings
and the international commerce somebody's making something

No this may be good enough for an old me but
IT
MUST
BE
BROKEN THROUGH

The new image will promise and deliver
Imagine the "new" New Haven city building rising a coruscated
broken arrowhead next to the gay gothic Henry Austin shell
for the new building shrouded in glass really comes
from an iceberg underground depth with swarms of earnest planners
Planners for a commercial cultural revival
not just jazz on the Green and ethnic foodstuff to tempt
the poor and the affluent alike but a new liveliness of
persons distributed from the underground planning warrens
threading their projects through the sick and dying <u>civitas</u>

provide conveying fanzine and fanac networks for renewed
neighborhood and block associations cultists of energy
old and young alike to share in nay batten on
hairstyles skirtlengths thirdworld jewelry food of universal
veggiegrain healthfulness like hamburgers for those who want it so

Most important rhythms will arise from still robotized forms found
everywhere especially Christmas office parties
one would think we'd simply borrow and blend with Blacks
but they too haven't been spared the sorrowmachine airwaves
so we'll have to reinvent rhythm and movement using of course

american forms to follow simply the heart's motion
darker wilder push from toes and soles groin plexus
not entirely missing the brain but not dwelling there long
but balancing fiery urges and the delicate thoughttouch
the result being new families defined by block and village

maybe there will be communal mystical links of Westville Spring
Glen Morris Cove Fair Haven all the colonial nodes surrendered in
my time to fast cars on boulevards and life-covering interstates
new tunes too will hold the street-men-women
at one with rentier seven figured surgeon idled computer analyst

Ay me I fondly dream sorrow not to be so fancifully undone
the ponderous bulldozers crush romance tasting envying
more and more a million beauteous astroturf
golfcourses styrofoam cups airconditioners unzipping the sky
return me to me poor poet following the bouncing cursor
waiting for internal heaven to rise descend and bless a poem

FLOAT

"To move, move, move, as an end in itself,
an appetite at any price"

~Henry James, *The American Scene*

I

I lay back, uncertain of all
but delight and fear intangibly mixed.
It didn't hurt that Mother held me,
not the fleshy but pleasant Father.
Loving and constraining presences,
the chief burden of this song,
this discourse, line of this riff.
How can I absorb the world evenly
when, as I pig out on its pleasures, all
grows piggish, sullen acceptance?

Thick covered in blackest mud, bobbing Dead Sea
gelatin eye to eye with undeviated blue.
The Holy Land welcomes me.
Melville, sunk in 19th century
squalor, answered with twenty thousand
lines. The waste places of dead end
ghoulish piety lit by his brooding light
over the Holy Sepulchre. What was I
to do on the oily waters no water
could thin out?

Dramatizing my watered down Jewishness,
yen for a universal Jesus shape,
me—yes, me as Jesus, why not?
Then messiahship would be collective
since anyone, even women, could be him.
So collective desires sugar
the biblical storybook home, yellow light,
robes and beards, long hair, flashing eyes.
The backlit story is father God's, eater
of people as sure as Moloch.

As this search meanders, shall I
scrap the dry byways of my past? Ours is
a story about push, a clot of tissues
come out of the sea, once swallowed,
given by ancient waters.

                    II

The frantic act setting down roots hoglike
in yesteryears. Recording provides us
with a story, the evermoving float,
the inner tube of childhood. To float enwrapped
in a caul of flesh through endless days, breaking
through like Puritans! When talking to a bank clerk,
I try to hold her eyes despite the feral look
of all our kind caught at a nervous angle.

Maybe pastoral distance, even animality,
fear of too much health makes me flee
to childhood tales of smoky caves and hermits.
To glide through tunnels of driveup bank shelters,
engine running, the chassis and tires
lifting me, the teller's amplified
voice and stiff hairdo disembodied...
a wonder I can handle car and or finance.
To ride on the springs of my Toyota,

hot day, interior cooled, windows tinted
against world's glare, far off traffic's grind
muffled by Billie Holiday's Body and Soul
on my tape deck, to feel jazz New York
clubby, to glide bluesily through the day's void,
to let drift jazz's fleeting sensual ache,
flip side of romance and untanned whiteness.
Yet country and city, fresh laundry smells,
country cooking, honeysuckle threading, sun
yellowing the kitchen floor—all nearly
illicit—billowed by Lester Young's
boozy riffs taking me home where
gods of velvet and cool shadow dwell.
Like in bed telling stories, singing songs
I wanted to know, wanted never to change,
print dresses, cereal boxes, radio families.
To float on, drifting through cities,
glancing off neutral eyes of passing
strange men and women, chances for encounter,
recording the image of flood.

III

To stretch... attached by a silver thread
to Edwardian romances, '30s movies,
a thread leading nowhere, looping
around and around a tight-woven spool
of shadow wishes. Tribes <u>are</u> important
and New York Expressionists laid on the flux,
giving background noise, pumping support
to the main lines. Most battles have been fought
in private, silence. Even a few chosen
muses remain unaware of their election,

afflatus longing for play and passion,
shifting to decorous solemnity.
All this time spent in worry, time choked waiting
at the station with one train a day, early 4 AM,
only three widows with blind astronomer.
"Body and Soul," we could say of each other,
"unless we could have one more chance."
"A hundred thousand flaws,"
choked accumulations blocked—what?—
I almost said the "flaw" of my feelings.

Floating now the passive compromise of
aggressive crawl, legs and arms flashing,
yielding easy water's comfort,
my will, defying flooding lungs in violence
of water's desire to fill my bulk.
Floating trusts to the water's motions.
All had knowing in our mother's bodies,
can recognize such motion now,
breathing slow and deep as the dark figure
approaches, we hope will be our mother.

KEEPING UP WITH IT

"We all agree it's too big to keep up with,
that we're surrounded by life,
that we'll never understand it..."

~Jack Kerouac, *Big Sur*

"Bring up the armor!" I woke up screaming,
not knowing—in the forgetting way of dreams—
what armor the dream referred to. I saw no
clear images out of the night fog.
Knight requesting his arming, swung onto a horse
as in Olivier's Henry? The dusky steel men
from the Cleveland Museum armory hall?

More likely George Scott as Patton calling up
the tanks in the Bulge, looking back to scorn
smirking reporters and a void of snow.
Images showing loss and expectation, and terror
of not having what I needed always:
a finely hammered carapace for the world's arrows,
piercing daily gargoyles of cold eyes.
That's the sort of graffiti left by my generation.
The syntax and sense are questionable but
the roil and rush could be what we wanted.
Wit cometh and goeth. So we're back where we
started from. Right back where we started from.
So little makes sense but language.

Partially scratch the above. Computer talk
and acts excite many in our time,
as baseball did only a few years ago.
Their welter of talk and stats and
functions calmed even the noblest of us.
Our great chests swelled, belying us
and trembling like first graders.
Phylacteries, too, are hard to jest about.
Starkness of any kind–in farmhouses,
Gallic faces, art nudes–can't take jests gracefully.
Beyond the rice pilafs and veggie hot dogs
one fears that his children's teeth will yellow
and rot because they don't have insurance,
or that retirement will pall more than work.

Such fears of times to come signal
a dish-washing mind, a house painting mind,
which some will say with kindness, demonstrate
a healthy immersion in the quotidian,
the twirling of a maple leaf.
After all, isn't this the stuff of Zen masters
raking pebbled walk ways, dusting the gong?

Such fears will fade, what counts
is the present, making do. Mediocrity
may triumph the here but there the past
still retains its golden flavor. After all
you've suffered, you deserve to relish
quietly the falling leaf.

You have grown accustomed to presences
beyond identifiable life parallels. I'm not
a New Ager. But you and I starry eyed circa 1821,
fervently embrace a new age.
The doomsters are *there* and might be as support
A Yahweh of Sinai and his accompanist, Jesus of Nazereth,
Or object to Muhammad's vision of angels,

They have vanished into legend, as soul
gathering hedges the former beliefs.
I mean the earthly presences most of us feel,
A cloud of guidance in the wind's breath,
certainty's surge. No doubt friend less, alone.
All things shrink as a yellowed newspaper.

Is anything truer than the sudden lock in of an eye,
time suspended while another's being is shared?

III

RUNNING

I don't know why I punished
my body like this at my age.
Every morning I drove to
the high school track
to grind out twelve turns.

I ached all day. Maybe my view
of curves and straights revived a
high-school desire to make the team,
running a staggered-lane 220,
me on the outside lane ahead,
for tenth of seconds hoping
I might win. Then the others
thundered by, cinders flying
from their swifter feet.
Story of my life.

Five decades later, I run on asphalt,
my legs still drag. Yet my
wind holds up. A breeze cools me
as I round the east curve,
stretching toward the end
where coldwater waits,
then knowing swift feet
also can be mine.

THUNDERBOLT

The late afternoon received it,
pure, blue, and swift, like Zeus
(named after the blue sky)
on a precise and violent,
another erotic mission. It missed us
to strike a fat man next door,
in a plaid bathing suited, blue sneakers
reaching for a transistor,
who none of us knew. It seems
the flash hit a pine tree, exploding
bark like popcorn, spiraling to ground,
two-forked, split a rock, drilling
his forehead.
Lost, to the cause of his death
While we scurried toward him.
He lay pot-bellied to the pine trees.

I felt his broad chest. No life.
I thought of his hysterical
widow inside, out of the weather.
I thought lightning always struck twice
(or was that the postman never, or
always, knocking twice?) I fixed
on a cauterized hole as if
staring at my double. (It was,
after all, only a matter of time.)
The bitch goddess Fortuna had done him
to a turn. As the darkening afternoon
sped around us, awaiting
our demeanor with his fat widow
and his funeral, he stirred,
rolled his eyes, and like Falstaff
on the battlefield, but utterly
witless, stood up, strangely
asked to know all of it. How could
we know causes? I wondered
abstractly about the nature
of thunderbolts, their myths,
their terrible ways.

We left the man to his weekend
miracle and cabin–all of us
were new from the city–
he now in disarray with gasping
embraces. We walked back to the
miraculous day at water's edge,
bathed in soft blue light.

ORIGIN OBSCURE

"...the shark, after all, is a professional survivor."

~W.S. Merwin

The Cousteaus, in love with the sea,
move with the shark in "respect,"
Philippe's word for the necessary

posture with a dangerous host
who apparently has roamed unchanged.
Cousteau tells us of his worship
as a benevolent god. Besides our
fascination with blood rites,
two facts make our terror interesting:
it sinks if it stops swimming,
it must swim continually to breathe.
Poor wanderer, it swims for its life.

It appalls us all, the name itself chilling the most
experienced diver, shadowing oceans,
inlets, beaches. In countless photos
the dark shape sunlight striped it moves
effortlessly with the sea, an efficient
machine made for nothing else but
killing in quantity, in silence,
in blindness, its senses eon-honed.

I find my terror ghosting me as
it breeds like a rabbit, all life moving
away around as we find our own
shadows in our forebears' sacrifices thrown
into a lagoon, feeding on offal, afterbirth
from dolphins, working its blind will
alone, gathering for banquets in frenzies
echoing our own collective violence.

His shape slides through my mind,
that other ocean where each kind
straight its own resemblance finds,
leaving morsels for the pilot fish,
wise parasites trailing after
endless swimming to other meals,
other seas.

THEM

*"...almost as fecund as germs... symbol of the Judas
and the stool pigeon, of soullessness in general."*
~Joseph Mitchell, *The Bottom of the Harbor*

We think, unadmiring, he had a rat like face,
what we see as we say, "he scurried."
In rats alley where dead men lost desire
before they lost their bones.
A book on them in history infects us
with hidden causes.
Shylock's mocking fear: his house is troubled with a rat.
Like rats that ravin down their proper bane.
A common cry at an innocent age: oh rats!
We can smell one.
We can drown them.
We can lead them out of town.
We can rhyme them to death if we're Irish.
We can be as them if we're Jewish.
A rat, a rat, dead for a ducat!
Every deserter or strike breaker.
To betray, to waffle, shuffle.
A scurvy politician gnaws our garners.
Without a tail, I'll do, we'll do, you'll do.
Their holes and pathways, so ingenious
where such hide and skulk.
Why should a rat have life and thou no life at all?
Praise be to all creatures who catch and rend them.
I saw two in the subway scaling the third rail:
how intent, how brave!

Encountering Henry Moore's Nudes in Public Places

I walked in mingled awe and boredom
among the casual swoop-hipped pinhead
mothers in glass museums of bluish summer.

Couldn't these fates have ordered better?
With ponderous mockeries I heard them:
"We squandered the arbors, stripped the topiary."

"He was such a sweet boy, always tending
his sickly brothers." "He delivered his papers
while also vastly admiring us."

Again arrived at the capitol of nudes,
I refuse to scare. I won't scrape, won't, won't.
Oh, their sly flippant gratitudes won't do.

They must pine for park-bench womankind,
slouched and sweaty with the kids, while greenhouse air
from the staid gardens passes in a wave.

I wait for them to undulate. Measured
forms should stir from slumbers in summer flare.
Their mental flesh glow in bronze than steel.

Will their dark language or rough-ridged hefts
give back a hazy stumbling past? I arouse
my nerve, call them to break the spell, vitrify

asphalt walks, eat up an acre, glide
into tangos, tune up their brassy anthems,
let their weedy sea scents spill.

MAD IN ITALY

In this steep Etruscan town
a tavern door frames
a man holding forth with air,
mild as the bittersweet drinks.
His phantom interlocutors
are forgiving in reproof.
Few of us notice. Many of his kind,
judged harmless, freeing the state of burden,
circle the spiralled streets.

Gold-toothed, thick-fingered,
short-cropped, scrubbed and stubbled,
he hovers before me.... I think of
Machiavelli, robed for his
day's study, quill poised,
prepared with fierce irony
to wield ancients against moderns....
The madman discourses
in the smooth-oiled Tuscan tongue,
hands lifted, finger pointing
to his clear contentions, as civil
as his ancient town.

Troubled sleep, no appetite,
tossing, sweating over mystic
texts, burning for every girl
outside in the piazza,
defrosted from monastic wards,
he now warms to his circling
and everlasting life. He smiles at
his intricate world of wheels
within wheels, now halted by his will,
now spun faster, faster to
the golden glowing of Giotto's angels
hovering over a Passion scene.

By the subtlest nod he changes
the traffic light, over and over –
green, orange, red, green...
bathing the soft stucco tavern
walls with an Umbrian palette's hue.
By his falcon-eager glance,
our talk livens then slows with
his quick-fallen pensiveness.

In a wing-beat I am lifted from
the tavern floor and put softly down.
The bartender winks, smiles.
Leaving, I look back to see
The freed wanderer sweetly point
through the night's soft mist
at spirits from fair Assisi
shimmering across the valley.

In Memory of Antoine de Saint-Exupéry

We shrug off glamor sometimes,
fearing the easy rush of words
like the unexpected caress.
Insidious, such a style,
like some cabaret songs
piercing the tough–edged brain,
unlocking memories asleep
in the closet corner for years.
Dusty, easy,
nostalgia's cigarette burned
sheen attracts.

Galactic flickers of a life
like this brave and curious man,
now forever antique among
the odds and ends,
have come to a country airfield
in a cool wind at night
where I hear, I feel the clear
solitary last flight,
the engine's drone, the soft
curve of the bowl of stars.

IV

BIBLE STORY

Jacob sums it up. For the teacher or scholar
everything makes sense, also a pretense of mystery
is kept up. The truth is, the old family,
unspoken in its resentments and favorites,
kept up its ways with herding, travel, local pacts.
Mother, father, two brothers, one grabbing
A heel in the womb, conspiring for the birthright,
the father knowing but doing nothing,
a mourner for the father who steeled himself
to slit his throat, the bewildered childhood the text omits.

He chose his mother's will
Lying–knowing his father knew–
and as a kind of double, wept, knowing himself
bound to Esau, whom he pretended to be.
We would make Esau the other.
He cannot be, for Jacob sought to be him.
Besides, they're brothers, yet so different.
Their mother was narrow eyed for the bright one,
the other freed to the fields of appetite,
the father long wearied by surrender.
And blood, rearing high and raging
for the marrow of the lives to come, will out.

Then Jacob bested the dark angel,
grasped the reward for holding tight,
divine travelers ascending and descending
between earth and heaven.
A show for him, specially granted.
How he envied them!

47

MORIAH
To the memory of Dennis Silk (1928-1998)

Tourists and pilgrims alike expect monuments will be
more grand or diminished than dreams and guidebooks tell,
and this great Mount rises as huge and fictive as Herod,
the wonder builder, courter of Roman and Jew.

Summer blue washes over this place, over
the black beards, green fatigues, white shorts
covered for piety with black garbage bags,
the gray and brown dust of ages only slightly shadowed
by the black building cranes perched like siege towers.

A polyglot crowd ascends the ramp, camera laden,
each serious or trivial in purpose, our guide trim,
cheerful, radiant as women tend to be in Jerusalem.
A few of us read a rabbinic warning, hesitate, decide
not to go, fearing the inept step on holy ground.
Going up exhilarates, the stretch of thigh and breath,
even this short haul to Abraham's hardest hour,
the servants left behind,
the voice still ringing his ears.

Tradition holds it as that place.
Looking out over this bazaar of a city,
at the monochrome landscape, the hotbrown hills
breathing heat, the olive grove dots, the white
villages, I see it as somehow the right unlikely place.

It is Ramadan and we're delayed until the mosques empty
of penitents, pilgrims. Piety surrounds
Jerusalem with a common and mischievous air.
The slim guide, a transplant here, deftly leads
her flock to various remnants, to the fortress where once
Rome's legion kept watch for rebellion below.

Touch and circling the dome's rock I notice the beauty
of thin Arab women, padding barefoot, low lidded,
heavy breasted through gauzy folds.
I watch them kneel, bow, touch foreheads to the Rock,
deep at the core. Children move awestruck over the carpets
and blue mosaics. Outside the sun strikes us all
with a strange carnival gaiety.
Smiles break over us like waves.

In the sea that is Jerusalem the ship lies drydocked,
half afloat, awkward in the sun's glare.
At night, in the wall's floodlights
the mount rights itself from yawing westward.
Going down I look along the wall for high water marks.
Remarkably, the disasters left a stone inscribed by a man
who lived on to have his hopes crushed.
May all our bones flourish like grass.

I think the dome on its rock, looks very like the
place to sacrifice sheep or sons,
the thigh pieces darkening the stone.
I wonder if the saving ram's bones were buried,
or just left to the sun?

I go lower to the bedrock that is Jerusalem
its limestone layers mocking the stones
perching on it, mute prophets, lifting them,
bearing its burden. I go farther through a tunnel's
buried stream called gushing Gihon,
"fast by the oracle of God,"
deeper into stone where stone was hewed.
My head aches with the weight of stone, the water's rush
and rock the city rocks in its stone waves,
the sun seeking all out in pitiless glare.

I flee up into the quarter where drinks
and warm bread await. Here on another hill,
higher then Moriah, I look down
on the domed Mount, its declivities
filled in by ambitious Herod,
the foreigner no one trusted.

GOD

stayed close to my boyhood,
became immanence in my
enthrallment with my world,
flush and shadow, the first hotness
of desire, then a cold retreat within.

remained insistent, became insistence:
unfathomable equations, history's roiling,
his posture on the Sistine ceiling,
a soaring elegant gentleman;
a refusal to play cosmic dice.

who kept no promises, fading
into my small events, colors, textures;
the measureless presence lost
from unknown angers.
I thought he would keep my promises,
keep all of them for us all;
in blazes, unfurled, save for believers on the march.

I dream myself back, waiting cold and wet,
emptied of small reasoning, acquired skills.
since lived by. The trolley pulls up,
packed with the world's hostile poor.

SLIDE SHOW

Remote East Friesland's upper reaches,
this landscape around Aurich, spreads out
a Hollandish scrub brown, a stretching sea,
fields streaked yellow green, low gabled
farmhouses pressing the earth, holding on tight,
a road aimed at the heart of north. Children
have drowned walking those flats, dreaming
low tide, some taken under in a sea rush
while parents in insect terror flee across
the dull flats as windmills hugely squat.
I half expect fourth–dimension fingers
to pinch off houses and squirming folk.

I squint at faces there, some brutish
potato faces, some well hewn,
in their remote parlor amenities
children of distance, stolid
as their great spotted cows.

A memory seeps, teases, reaches for
stories of great grandparents come in
a sailboat "from the north of the old country"
to stitch shoes in a big red factory
on the river ("looked like the state pen"),
Ohio hicks, sticking leather, scrubbing sidewalks,
singing in the *Arbeiterchor*. The Aurich
folk could be half mine. My other half,
Galician *Jüden*, pressed in, then ripped loose.

By a flash on the magic screen, at the synagogue site,
an apology engraved for "our neighbors taken away,"
shattered with the wedding glass.
Rough limestone juts in menace
from a petunia bed, joining fields, sandbars–
all in the tidal push, while trucks dump
muckloads to keep the gray sea's damages at bay.

LATE NOVEMBER

Close to your Roman birthday, Jesus,
I wonder after all these years how you gawked at
the warren of Jerusalem, bumpkin from Fanaticville,
way out, weird eyed, locust lipped,
talmudically inclined in an odd country way.

I'm not writing your elegy, for Christ's sake,
I, a middle-aged middling Jew,
who just yesterday sighed
and thought you out again.
I can't get your haloed, bleary-eyed
look out of mind, knowing if I know you
looked more like Arthur Garfunkle,
smelled of fish oil, licked your fingers,
and did the old Midrashic tricks,
clever and wiser than most.

You looked saddest on the road to Emmaus,
Rising like a vacant rock star before the little rabble.
Better than the Cross, myriads preceding
While myriads followed.
To this day, strange master, you have wept.

Never of your faith-to-come, I too am trapped
in the present's warren, fire at one end, sticks at the other,
heaving for air.

ENTRANCE TO THE OLD CRACOW GHETTO
(After a photograph by Roman Vishniac)

Symmetry of alleyways and courtyard arches
caught his harried eye, and mine.
Appia and Reinhardt dreamt the massive planes,
the rainslicked cobblestones. Such shabby weight
comes from the newsreel's black and white country
of hunching men and eternal sleet,
a monumental texture in ruined places,
overcoats grey shapes.

Like Isaac they knew nothing.
Indifferent through the crosshatched streaks,
they bend toward railed upper walks.
A perfect photograph, shadows clicking into place.

One climbs stairs, upper right,
toward a mumbled prayer, a cold meal,
a broken business.
Little wine or oil of the promised good land,
the yellowing Silesia beyond his eye.
Yet a foggy grace soars from pillars.
A dove preens into my sight.
A bent shadow certainly will turn
to spring the cage,
plunging the bird into a shining field.

READING THE TALMUD

Three A.M. In the soul's dark,
Scott Fitzgerald said,
It's always this time.

The close gloom cast on my grandfather.
Clean shaven, his suit impeccable,
He must have known of the Talmud.
The endless inserted texts, multiple life
Vignettes. Pynchon details.
They blind me yet I read it at random,
Alone late at night in English.

All matters given strange importance.
What prayer to say on opening a closet door
Or what cow wandered into a neighbor's field.

Why attend to what will always be
Dark to me, games like pinochle, dominoes,
Not lost but still holding me bound.

A FAMILY ROMANCE

I thought by this late date to have arrived
at the bright diner where mother and father
happily in constant habit settled the bill.
At home pillows wafted their plumped scent,
the beach path curved neither too near nor far.
thoughts of abduction from such primal bliss

to the hard sell, tax forms—all anti-bliss—
swirled ominously as dark clouds arrived.
I planned to keep, what on the absurd far—
field abstract level remained: my father,
a promised fishing trip, his leather scent
after a hot country drive, every bill

paid. Calmly we waited for Uncle Bill,
as his presence blocked our customary bliss,
while baseball wafted its fresh green scent
lightened us before the man arrived.
While in sweet expectation, against father
and his easy pitches, I hit hard and far.

The family flashed and flared, so far
past our incidental power to bill
us. I thought all payable by father.
Our mandate of heaven, promised bliss
of Kung and disciples. Mine hadn't arrived,
as Mom said, "family duty." His scent,

pungent like earth, that warm enriching scent,
kept family harmony not far
from ballpark harmonies... yet not arrived
with cool, calm movements but like a wren's bill,
frenetically poking bugs in bliss.
This hammered home our secret fear: father

and his uncertainties. For father,
mother hinted, held feeble sway. Her scent
suffused the subtle rose and violet bliss
all through the house's wards and confines–far
past heaven's mandate. For Uncle Bill
would darken us to our depths when he arrived.

Uncle's rancid scent clung on us all, a bill
~~well~~ *far* beyond what we could pay, mocking bliss.
To suffocate father, his brother had arrived.

NEW FACES

Clocks never struck so thunderously
or kept such illusory absolutes
as when this digital glitters in Time's eye.

Once more consider clocks. Like nimble
young stock clerks, the second hand
sweeps the minute clean while two brothers
pass the business on to shiftless sons.

On their stern faces we once saw
a Roman phalanx, Sleep and Wake,
knights–with–maces, ecstatic cherubs,
or, more lately, elegant needles and dots.
Inviting us for a ride on stout arms,
they kept us waiting for a creaking moment,
as a Ferris wheel would perch and rock,
in our majestic, aching view of the midway.

On the town square's clock might appear
in bronze and stone stern maxims against torpor;
or announce the dreadful hour, instructed
by pictures, while we welcomed the rigor
of numbers, lonely, in pale formation.
Those faces prompted us to tell in leisure,
to see before and after, while a robed guide
pointed to the yawning chasm below.

With patience and poise these stern faces kept
our hours, marked our boredom and fear,
ruffled or smoothed our repose, showed
us the door, or laid out an ancient map
to plan tomorrow's long journey,
after they showed us clean beds for the night.
But now new lines glow in story-less, limit-
less road–marked stripes, new stone-eyed guides
whose benumbing glowing makes certain
we know them as our better, cleaned-up act:
"Now. Another. Nothing will change."

COSMOLOGY LESSONS

Ever since childhood's vast spaces
I've thought about infinity,
mind and flesh.
(The child remains our
natural philosopher.)
The innocent and aching romance
in later life returned,
with settlings and botches.
The stars are unimaginably
remote, yet consolable.
Our universe, that very name,
a caul of blackness,
sickened and chilled
my budding sexual warmth.

What's troubling is the pull
away from world and flesh
out toward floating ice and fire–
or gravity's steady state of gravity
in planetary life.
Like the life of others,
the huge wheel turns me
into a whirling cycle toward collapse.

SANDS OF IWO JIMA

Strange heroes I had, Agar and Wayne,
reticent and smoking while tracers whined;
one private, glowering, the other
caustic macho, never an inept move,
quick with bootcamp wit, a vicious
punch waiting to be pulled.

A gang of us dug in behind my house—two trenches
in suburban fields a bounding in '44.
Our mothers hoarded sugar, we gathered
booty from our fathers' and uncles' war,
nesting Krauts in July, Japs later.

What a kit we had! tiny files for barbed wire,
An uncle's edible aviator maps, pocket periscopes,
Jungle–blotched greens, dud grenades,
helmets with real rasping chin straps,
an ancient Zenith with crooner tunes
for digging by. Tunneling through the hot
day, we dug deep and wide:
crawled, spied, held fast,
stripped, bronzed marines.
Deadly with Model P-51's and
Zeroes we hoarded in fox holes in private
caches discovered by a lunatic among us
who bombed the dog house hangar after breakfast.
Fair was fair. To give up a lacquered
Zero to a bully crew cut, to pick miserably
at the delicate torn wings, not knowing
the battle led nowhere but to splintered balsam
and sniggering. But time fell gently on
sweatiness and dangers, calls to lunch,

girls ignored; hiding hairless bodies
from big heinies and lurking japs
kept all our sweaty labor and joy.
In the end, Wayne bought it; Agar slogged on,
taught hardness by the lovable giant tough guy:
inheriting irony in disordered line
behind sandbags, patience and despair
while we flipped away our Lucky Strikes.

America, how safe you were with us
in those long afternoons fortifying
our positions, how nearly tangible
the ack-ack and the tracer, the mortar's
sullen thump, the bayonet's perfect slot
in the mock M-1!

V

A Life Pinched by Circumstance

We begin to see
our endings
at a gray moment
in a field awaiting
the far-off shout
or by the rush of sound
and sharp points of light
through an ill-remembered dream.

Sometimes the morning light
withholds even these visions
forcing a return
to shadows.

Notice how while peeling
an orange the gentle tearing
the reluctance of rind and fruit
to part.

All the coverings of his life
won't easily be severed
from the dream of it
the shining flesh within.

At the Desk

A solid place to be, as if all things
sat perfect, rectangular. Though moved
at least a dozen times, it's rooted now
to a good oak floor, with a swivel chair
and me sometimes animated fixtures.

Platonists tell of a deathless,
shadowy Table, to me magically in–
substantial. But the logic of
commandeering connections
to countless earmarks here below
(like this shadow on my second floor)
makes sense, moves me. Like a math
problem that first fogged then flashed
clear in a little blaze, its utility sits well.

As for details,
I point to the seven cracked drawers,
three on a side, the shallow middle one–
a dull symmetry–plus their sad brass
ring pulls. Within: tax records;
foolscap pads; chipped-gold paper
fasteners, mounted specimens
on faded cardboard; shiny Bics alongside
an ancient nib; in abandoned birthday
wallets molder photos, one of my
dead father supplicating
through clouded cracked plastic.

These and other things I won't discard
though I've started, hoping a
cleanout, even another desk–
a shining vast table, no drawers–
could clear my life, bring the art
I want. But here I am with hieroglyphic
nicks, like those forgotten bottom-drawer
poems, signatures of whatever this
dumb squat thing may store.

Any sign, any hint of Plato's Deluxe Model?
Or at least some answer to your query,
What goes on here?
Mostly sitting.
On occasion a neck–kinking snooze,
Window–gazing on weather,
or mailman, or the sidewalk kids,
or the street lamp holding out.
A lengthy sit most mornings,
some evenings, with car swish, birdsong,
TV babble clouding somewhere,
or the boy down the street who slams
the car door, grinds off in a rage.
Mostly waiting. In annoyance,
or bliss, near rage sometimes myself
for the underground fire of memories,
trusting one or two
will burrow through this mess,
find the right pen.

THE SHAPE OF DESIRING

"Yes, why shouldn't I be happy,"
cried a man in shabby green
slumped over coffee in a dark part of town.
And so it was. His life was changed.
The remarkable conversion thus begun,
the street into which he walked
brimmed pert and brilliant:
men in holes, women in flashing carts,
miraculous dogs leaping at winter,
the baker man crisp at his clanging trays,
all trades alive to the hour,
awash in subterranean sound.

The green man took up the watch
at the corner where all the past flashes.
How delicate the motion by his new light
where a girl glides soundlessly by.

OHIO TOWNS

The drive on state routes made for farm
commerce arrows north as though
the car was a feather in the sky stretch.
I forget what I'm driving for.
In the mind grows a boy's farm summer.
I'm pleased with my essential America,
its blue sky, white shingles, glimpses
of a sun labor left untouched.

That man in his tractor, will he have the farm next year?
People do care about their towns.
The bird's call, the rural crossroad,
the scorched abandoned silo,
a mingling of the present and
a coming time that goes for money.

In the white light between Ashland and Wellington
lay my life, one of a heartland multitude
gone to cities, barns sagging behind them.
Connecticut church fronts,
Victorian town halls still usable.

Little change, straight and potholed
as fifty miles become fifty years.

The meadowlark knows nothing but its own song.
I forgot what I came for
yet the light is telling me.
 I flash by an Amish couple in a carriage.
What is it that makes these things themselves?

Under these skies I had hoped
for infinity. What I got instead
was a red barn and a rusty tractor.

HOUSEBOUND

A GARDEN

A troubled dream, deep buried
in a careful garden plot,
squarely weeded and staked.

Uneasily held, after long searching,
felt for crab grass, misplaced fescue,
squeeze of invading beetle.

Knowing good & evil here,
time warps as tomatoes whiten, yellow,
redden toward my grasper hand.

Four kinds of lettuce
rise and wave in short triumph,
quick-bolting in the sun.

A HOUSEPAINTING

Pressed to shingles, the ladder
slips if I'm not careful.
Keeping order the skill here.

Scrape, prime, the glossy coat,
wine thin, no good. Thick as blood,
cottage red here in New England.

Set against white trim, I'm deep
wounded from this red painting,
worth it for shine, renewal sense.
Now the cleaning up, the good smell,
holding me house-wise to the grain.

TO THE SHOPS

Something must be done again,
words have stopped, so it's up
and out to civil clusters.

Old Irish men on the street
fancy being old, putter like me,
eyes cagily cocked for cracks and leaks.

I fancy a long coffee, long cigar,
corner chat, plainness,
bright cars a few feet away, gliding.

A frenchified food shop
just moved in, pinewood shiny.
Hardware store, bright labels.

NEW ENGLAND GREENS

A pun, of course. My town
hasn't one, though colonial.
Only a "center," daffodil ringed.

The flag rope bangs its pole,
an irritant for the idle looker.
New asphalt steams the corner.

An accountant I know nods
as he crosses. Behind, a flush
on the high breasted girl's face.

Other centers, truer greens,
spread common, keeping out
rabble, roller skating,

EATING

All the garden, despite a brave show,
is finally good for,
plus meat and bread.

These I take a lively
lust in, growing and choosing,
complements to shop goods.

Red steak, well drained fries,
cold white wine (can that stuff
on red with meat, it's summer).

I force myself to devour slowly.
Light fades as I clean my plate.

THE LONG JOURNEY

Goethe needed ten hours
sleep, some say five is enough.
A houseguest awakes fitfully rested.
Of late I think too much of sleep,
have taken to tossing, gazing
at my eyelids' milky way.

GUIDEBOOK

1

In Kansas City, a famous ten mile fifty yard paved creek commemorates Boss Pendergast's victorious interest in a cement company. Aged fourteen, I ride my Sears–mail order bicycle its entire length and back, testing Pendergast's arrogant monument. The day is perfect blue–hot. I travelled long, I returned, I offer libation with six shots of my father's best whiskey.

2

New York Irish bars called Frank's or Mooney's draw me like walks in drizzle. Columbus at 106th holds me captive. Wood dark and greasy, glasses polished bright. Talk sullen, boggy, red-nosed, threatened by Puerto Rican storefront church. On the sixth day, I am asked to quote verse. I head for the dark door. Hopper should be here to get the winter west side light shafts that pierce me as I leave.

3

Remembering big days, Venice gives me stage sets.. I sit through a day of cheap beer in St. Mark's square grandeur now "charm," the yellow lights on poles, the elegant man and woman at the next table, the celebrated decay of our imaginations. I leave a tip and walk deep into the mild night. A thousand crafted bridges keep me dreaming while I walk over dark water.

4

Jerusalem has the past bonding everyone uneasily. Golden stone, clearly-remembered current events. Zion Square is now a huge hole for a new hotel. A nearby street of Turklike shops sleepily opens wrought iron doors in the morning. The Levant calls for early meditation. I spend it reading the world's English press as the proud sun climbs once more. Later I move down a narrow street for sunset and a golden local wine.

5

I have decided to sit but not to weep by New England's pleasant ponds. Trying for permanence, I give common ducks stale bread. The whoosh of far off traffic is muffled. I have begun to study penmanship and my own past.

A SUMMER SONG

"All my winner's luck is done"
(calls starling to sparrow).
"Worm's in the ground, won't out now."

"My song claims all the hereabout"
(sparrow lightly taunted)
"and your sweet labor's now for nought."

Spring rain's spent, June's sucked dry,
the mole turns certain in his earth,
grass roots bind yet he finds his way.

Air pulses the summer earth,
sun rolls sunny side up with care,
spongy depths push as I walk.

All fall easily, turn the trick of tide:
Adam, Lucifer, Humpty, Wall Street,
all come rushing in a rebus flood.

HEATWAVE

Massive shape celebrates
bronze gong before forsaking.

Hard to know if an enormous
Hand can ring or abstract jaws
Will gobble the sky's cold fruit
and spit the seeds.

A street lamp centers me
me *here*, not *there*,
a point on a sky map.

Not that bulk,
whose slow draw on life's juice,
cellular half shadow,
probably has my number.

Coldly I wonder at the moon's
fabled disruptions, maidens ruined,
my heated life burning and spattering,

as perfectly in line, on time,
she readjusts our days.

CENTRAL PARK, 1972

Sycamores peel like Hiroshima victims,
rasp and branch into arthritic angles,
mottled pigeons march, circle my bench
with robot certainty.

Vague in memory's urgings, I stumble
to the sad sloped bench rest. Sepia
phantasms of a hundred Atget
photos smolder through my emptiness.

With other park loungers I avoided talk.
We looked unexpecting, no exchange.
A decade back I bounded from the bus
to relish the sheltered red-clay courts.

The late Victorian clubhouse welcomed us
like Ellis Island. Players stripped their suits,
donned whites, waited for a partner,
played serious two-hour matches, joying in
the pastoral release the city can give.

All cannot be the same, yet all is the same.
Time has not stained the pressed whites
of the sinewy regulars. Soaring above
Central Park West, twin undisturbed Royals,
old layered Art Decos, still rule.

Farther in the park, on an arched Venetian bridge,
the shadow of two casual tennis friends
in photos till strike poses like the thirties' movies,
an overexposed pallor fixed in my album.
Sycamores preside, blotched and comforting.

MAN WITH GLASS OF WATER

Simplicity always
asserts itself, never begging,
though the man on a street corner,
with tangled hair and dried sweat
captures passers-by
in a kind of violent declaration,
a gashed self. ~~Defence~~,

He is an arc covering everyone
hurrying back to desks, or lunch.
He has this thick green tumbler
of clear water. Styrofoam cups
blow everywhere in blind gutters.
In his encrusted hand the glass a rough diamond,
a coruscating beacon, seeming to say

"I offer anyone whatever of me
you want from this darkly shining
glass, the thing, the thing contained,
or like jewels from deep cool earth,
or water's depth from which bright spirit
flows, while August close cups us
in blasted trees, burning rubber, bus stops."

"I release you from all this, through sand
refined, from the panhandler's dark mind,
from the long day's downward pull.
From me, hands know ribbed calm certainty.
I give the moment, make it hold a day
in its rough reflection while refuse
clutters its dusty swirl, refining."
A shrivelled old woman proffers him

a Bosc pear. With grave deliberation
he bites into the bulge of hard brown fruit.
Through his pleasure I see a dusting of snow.
On dogwood branches the warm sparrows
dance, the sidewalk pigeons strut, a curb
harbors gathered watchers.

CAPTIVES

Through the corridor shines complete
liberated form. The David, youthful,
thrusts out and up, balanced, an arrow.
All that falls downward, his conquered Goliath,
out of sight.

In the corridor approaching him,
in shadows, four captives struggle still
with their stone, serenely encased,
limbs stuck in the thick of formed formlessness,
gripping at air. They search toward
the completed form of David, the young
whole one, light as they would be.

The gangway, green paint peeling, automated cell doors
whirring, blockhouse tiers squatting in midst
of yard, towers, guards, guns, razor wire.
The laundry with messages passed,
the mess hall's battered tables,
bored and acned guards.
Pale muscled men, scarred law books,
long-memorized routes to the town bar,
the pay phone, the girl, the cheap suit, the crisp money,
the noisy, delicious expanse of city and road,
the parole's intricacy.

Nothing suffocates yet flies free
like two seeking each other through other lives.
no solitary, no slitted food door like
that with others.

Waiting for the postcard
from the ex friend, ex wife,
for the yard's calibrated workout,
contraband fingered, map through the swamp.
He tries to lose focus on her long wait.

She moves through her life, veiled, shadowed
from him, him from her, puppets in a theater
closed for summer, their lives a sad rush
of leaves through abandoned city parks.

They bask together in a sun filled winter,
separate, excess of lives built, acquired,
for protection... layers of things
cushioning lives battered in unknown search.

Now it's oxygen from the same tank,
Buddy–breathing for the long ascent,
nothing but masks, watches, rubber suits.

Endless cocktails, village greens,
the suburb's rush in cars sealed
from everyday air, in sealed planes,
fear choked, to expensive places
assuring them that they've arrived–

while another longing circles them,
mars their customs, speaking of flesh ache,
sweet word rhythms, simplicity of gesture,
of their voices' truest music reaching, tuning
the unknown other to a warm circle of knowing,
of garden soil, colors, scents.

Nothing said. Years slide...
A meeting, an intonation, a glance,
small awakenings, nights as waitings.
Her dark head in a nimbus of dreams
and sweet flesh clearing the choking air.
The long dive for their treasure
in shocked joy, part in fear of paying the price...
Solitary, short rations, no exercise.
They crawl in a daily round
filled with glimpses, messages,
breathless calls, a hurried touch,
knowing any stretch of time
will be devoured in a second,
exhausted with their own fire.

For now, it's their time in the Yard,
notes passed in the laundry,
skills learned in the shop
to be used in parole time way off.

Banality of prisons, excitements
and disillusionments of visiting days,
pretended love, almost love, with others,
promises no longer pleasures,
ache and absence of the lifer,
waiting for the fifty dollars, the cheap suit,
the parole office, the fast food kitchen.

The captives pull and twist,
their yearning toward David,
his young perfection
twisted in emerging form. Like lovers
lonely in their separate suffocation,
they stretch out for time's running band
of light, time's stretch before them.

LINES WHILE DRUNK

The eager motions, rubbed and greened,
of the spring garden's upward thrusts.
A newness even in the peeling paint.
Ecstasies of wishing with the stuck record
that I too might be on the track.

The complexity of words spins,
and sentimental images ripen
into harmonies of requiems.
All is forgiven.
Every thief slumps at the bar of my desire,
every high school buddy—forgotten names—
an Odysseus in rags, kicked by the IBM
personnel man, the checkout girl, his wife.

Machines and foul fumes ascend
for purifying.
All flushes pink, sweaty with honest country labor.
Hardy's wonderfully—bosomed Tess
still walks the silent Dorset roads.
A rhythm I hear, a rhythm that some piper god,
local, lusty, reddened has flung to the harvesters
beats in my head, drives me to think,
just maybe, my head is not unclouded.

THE IVORY GATE

Two gates for ghostly dreams there are: one gateway
of honest horn, and one of ivory.
Issuing by the ivory gate are dreams
of glimmering illusion, fantasies,
but those that come through solid polished horn
may be borne out, if mortals only know them.
(*The Odyssey*, Book 19, trans. Robert Fitzgerald)

The scene is careful black and white,
vintage Rossellini, a dream
the beggar in us has, cunning,
lice-infested, drifting, where
our treasured self has left
its court to the clown. Perhaps
a crow perches on a flaking cornice,
or in a ravaged temple's sanctum,
or over a vomit-spattered portico.
(Decisions can be made on the set.
Keep the carpenter on hand
for fast changes.)

Experienced drunks should know better
than to try for handouts here,
where whores with wide black mouths
spit indiscriminate curses.

The set can be polished or left
as dead level as playing poverty,
as improbable as the current androgyny.
Mists flood in, caressing us
but giving no promise of sanity, truth,
or even the stability the local boss can give.

"You may never wake up," an actor whispers.
A huge black locomotive glides off set.
A Brueghel cripple draws
an inner curtain revealing sots
mimicking sex, a drooling minstrel
bent over a ukulele mocking
Picasso's blue man.

Out
~~A~~ hero rubs big swollen muscles,
tight and trembling at early waking–
He awaits the stringing of the bow,
ready to let fly the last of desire's arrows.

The White Coldness of this Spring

Little gets through as promised,
yet strangely I'm not saddened.
The sun disperses cleanly, trained
to pierce the hemlock, dogwood,
cold-shocked forsythia
bending groundward.

The sky net catches and floats.
Bizarre how I suddenly notice,
then forget how the sky moves
(we move of course), reminding
Me of fluent streams and days.
No matter when I notice,
nothing remains the same.

The elm through my window,
fungus ridden, has numbered
its withered and ripe years,
struggling through each spring's
leafing, now become, while crying,
"my last," yet dwindles, sending
his tracery roots under the street,
branch turnings casting webs
on a red house, blue car,
graying sidewalk.

The sky's thin palette washes
the grave air, mixing the gritty and pellucid–
such shyness to be born, to be green,
to thrust with new fiber.

The maple twists, yet in carapaced ease,
Sensing what to hold,
what to waste in twig and leaf.
I hold on to what flew in a cry over a wall.

"SO CLOSE TO HEAVEN..."

for Amy

"Unearthly "–sometimes the named
state for hovering, flying
close to blessed or unhallowed
ground, above it, looking down.

For me, earth places us where
we should settle, roam, gaze, seek
what we might have found at last
year's venturing out... as at

a distance, on a snow blown street–
as out of my own child life–
you met me and we bore the storm
stinging our faces on our journey home.

VI

SEPARATIONS

When closest, a lip away, fragrance
of curled washed hair, distance now
abstract, shapeless oceans swaying far

under black space, streaking stars, then the Others
smile, with the long teeth of their claims,
with what we thought we too knew, sweeping us out.

The remembered drawn-out label-words
half-spoken to everything half-loved,
misreadings, misfeelings, here at us now.

Treacherous voices, hatched and planned,
speak for our dreams, we, who keep flesh
so close, almost as if recalling our birth's pain.

Slow healing, the scars faded strips,
our animal creases keeping us in mind–
the hot ripping from old to perilous new.

FREEZE

Holding on to the car's edge,
near to slipping into a deep freeze
gripping me through an ice age,

knowing I just missed
a broken ankle
a wrenched back, a bruised hip

a month in a ward where you
can't bring me tea
or your gazing
or the length of your wrist
and few words–

But I'm safe for a moment
in the car taking its time starting
while I'm slipping and sliding
toward you.

THE WAIT

Turning to salt I end day's acrid
gunmetal I root down in asphalt cold
pretending to read–Jack Donne poems–
nodding to incurious passersby,
dully finished with classes and offices
still you do not come...

Ten minutes now knowing, multiplying
Minutes, freezing suffocating certainty,
High–lit order in a world of meetings,
my own grayness burns me.

It is not them. It's you burning me.
Where all was patience on her monument,
you fired me not only with martyr-flame
but propellent of the arsonist's skill.

For you I've shredded charts
buried compass staff and Loran
all the logs all plans all say they go by
for our days' raw green dawnings.

Here I am–fool's fever sweat in a pillory.
leering mocks scald my gashes
with each banal greeting I banal them back,
smiling with twisted petty mouth,
hideous the self without us.

For now I'm through.
I'm for warm beer cheery talk.
I grub for the car key.
Out of a shadow, a tower, a pillar of fire,
as quick as a rabbit's shivering in wet air
you're here.

POSSESSED

You recall the engorged lover before
he threw away his jewel-wife?
How he loved "not wisely but too well"?

Beneath those words, true and false, recall
when you felt the needle thread your skin,
lurid in your sleepless night:

the room of five hundred dream faces,
wisps of those past now acid
sucked in shock from a pipette,

bile rising, etching your throat,
or choking on a small sharp bone,
or lost dog nuzzling foreign doorsteps.

Out in a night of soaked blankets,
the press of strangers, half knowing you,
solemn, your heat rising, the damp

eating your secret flesh.
Neither accustomed nor dear place–
Nowhere–can harbor you tonight.

THE PARTY

Think me an alien who passes for a moment
relishing the insider talk–

Who's Who at the head of Which Bank,
which son barely made it through Yale.

Smug privilege, old and new money here
speaking the code everyone nods to but me.

Poor old me. Then I see you, all in black,
floating over the shabby glitter,

toward me, cowering at the center, our secret
speech rushing in a swift stream from your lips.

THE LESSON

*"For truly, I say to you, whoever gives you a cup of water to
drink because you bear the name of Christ,
will by no means lose the reward."*
(Mark 9:41)

A woman in a fine white church
keeps her habit of weeping there.

She doesn't know the cause of measured tears.
Perhaps the calm perfections

of a country life built on sound mergers,
buyouts, all the right times and places,

the bland gushings of any people
gathered to joy in their good fortunes–

All so different from her darkling passion.
Or, perhaps more simply, deeply, likely,

she longs to grasp his words, live his lesson,
to turn and offer a wild-eyed stranger cool water

in this white church–to take the burden of ~~this~~
those words, as she now smolders with them–

casting herself on some Mediterranean shore.

THE DOOR

She is a door
opening for me.

Through it spills light
I've never looked for.

It radiates, illumines,
touches with soft heat,

like the small, yellow sun
at the edge of winter's ending.

This light trembles with shades,
pulses with every season's colors,

like his God's living rays Dante
saw at the end of his voyage,

even here through the earthy
filter of her warm autumnal fire.

DYING

When I almost lost it then got it back,
someone asked what I saw "on the other side"
or words to that effect, or, I think half jesting,
"Did you see a white light?"

With a relief I can't remember,
lacking invention, I said I saw nothing,
felt nothing, though dully aware of being awake,
"happy to be here," adoring my thirst.

Happy, aware–not quite what a return
from the dead should be, with psychic
testaments blinding pre-believers into little
Pauls stumbling to Damascuses for birth.

Now leaks back from this ICU man,
how he yearned to stretch his little life,
at least so Scottie might beam him to a raised life.
I only saw your almond-shaped face telescoped

through a bandage tunnel, rehearsing
what I thought I knew but couldn't untangle,
if only because I smelled your skin, I began
to sketch a path toward unborn days.

THE AFTERLIFE

I want it to be just like this one,
and—here's the unoriginal part—

better. Of course, the better will
rage with selections:

I want her as she first was,
hesitant and thin, yet, clothes off,

fuller than promise itself.
I want our meals simple, gracious,

pasta or red steak, wine in good crystal.
I want her yearning as fresh as now,

as mine, mine as hers, each
racing with each other a mile off,

any discords wispy memories, awkwardness
her grace, that other life, an afterflush.

A CONDO IN SUMMER

The place we could end with
after the fearful certainties
in motels and parking lots,
quiet as we imagined,
disasters gathering now
at our foreign houses
we dreaded to go back to.

Here in a hot country calm,
a child-like bird call
we can't identify.

For me, classic rereadings,
the *Iliad*'s oddly comforting terrors,
the contorted peace of *The Brothers K*.
I reread my long-ago poems
surprised that I wrote at all.

You leave late to work in your office,
Then return to me, me like an old-time wife.
We dart like small deer,
sometimes or just out of control,
in recall of tearing away
for stretched-out weekends,
to rip out old growth, watch the new,
then and now bushwhacking Time,
gathering-rosebuds sprees,
drinking deep from mossy wells.

At deep night we hear the Interstate thrum
in unremitting undercurrent.
Sleepless, we rise to cook pasta,
watch a Fellini movie, try walking like
Giulietta Masina aloud,
collapse again like beached fish.
Against our mock-sober judgment,
we stagger again into our lists.

Thus spent, our days and nights cry bliss, yet
in an underthrill that life can't give us only this,
the flaming brand at Eden's edge
flaring through the soft dark.

FROM THE CATALOGUE OF TASTES

I have tasted:

Bread, holding you crisp, warm or cool, rising in my mouth,
or flat in the Passover matzoh, some covered,
some shown to all, one hidden, always my mouth
moist from the oven of your plainness.

Meat, your fat and muscle shocked from the sacrificial knife,
darkest of all savors, I as temple priest
ordained to hold, tear, gnaw you.

Wine, I savor you as fruit of the vine,
gathered from rich earth, warm sun, and labor.

I set this down while I am still of the earth,
not yet dispersed in unremembered ashes,
to desert wastes, greenest valleys, hovering mountains,
or when mingled in my mouth with the blood of sacrifice.
I am blessed in flesh while hunger gives over to savoring.
Saltness, sweetness, bitterness of the grape's,
bread's, meat's gross or subtle settlings on my tongue,
however far from fibrous rootedness in soil, of sun's heat,
or violent or gentle washing of soil by water,

All these lead me to mingle them from my body's
filigrees and webs, and from your hair, mouth, throat,
plain of belly, thighs, valleys,
as the earth, the sun, in continual motion,
sentinels to our bones' complicity,
drifting to thoughts, to the ambient air,
to the nothing awaiting the annihilating fire.

SENSES

Sound
      Your bell voice's lift and dip, slipping

Down, holding on a quaver, as you

Sight
      Gaze through distance at autumn's

Gold with gold glazing in your eyes.

Touch
      Your hand smooths sun warmed cotton,

Hair of my arm, parch of my lips.

Smell
      Your pine leaf bed springs up, as

Rosemary rubbed breath hovers,

Taste
      As tongues graze in throats' hollows,

As dough sweetens under honey's flow.

Beyond
      Beyond, guarding these ripenesses

We sense rarest air drifting far,

Steady, unseen, sustaining, free.

ABOUT THE AUTHOR

This collection of poems, written for over forty years, embody my inner emotions and outer experiences. Many of these poems have appeared in national literary magazines. Over that time I have taught English and American literature at Syracuse University, Washington and Lee University, and Quinnipiac University, from which I am an emeritus professor. As a scholar and critic, I have published *Stage and Image in the Plays of Christopher Marlowe*, co-edited *Selected Essays of Delmore* Schwartz, and many critical essays and reviews. I continue to write poetry, short stories, and plays. I am also a painter. I live with my wife, Betsey Parlato, in Tucson, Arizona.

Made in the USA
San Bernardino, CA
27 April 2016